43212-2000

Grandview Heights *and* Marble Cliff, Ohio

AT THE TURN OF THE MILLENNIUM

43212-2000

Grandview Heights *and* Marble Cliff, Ohio

AT THE TURN OF THE MILLENNIUM

Ken Frick - Photographer

Marble Cliff, Ohio USA

2000

Ken Frick - Photographer

1600 Roxbury Road

Marble Cliff, Ohio 43212

E-mail: CAM1600@JUNO.com

Editor: Cynthia A. McKay

Designer: Mike Dexter, IDC Design Group, Inc.

Paper: Potlatch Vintage Velvet

Printer: Hopkins Printing

LIBRARY OF CONGRESS CATALOGING-IN-PUBLICATION DATA

Frick, Kenneth D., 1948-
          "43212-2000 Grandview Heights and Marble CLiff, Ohio at the turn of the millennium"/by Ken Frick. - 1st ed.
                    p.256 cm. 21.5
              ISBN 0-9708372-0-8 (pbk)
              I. Grandview Heights (Ohio)--Pictorial works. 2. Marble Cliff (Ohio)--Pictorial works. 3. Photography.
              II. Title

Printed in the United States of America

I set out to document my community at the turn of the millennium.

And what I found were people of character and people who are characters.

We are truly blessed.

KEN FRICK

January 1, 2001

For my wife, Cynthia, and our son, Kevin,

my mother, who would have been so proud,

and all my neighbors.

43212-2000

Grandview Heights *and* Marble Cliff, Ohio

AT THE TURN OF THE MILLENNIUM

"My grandfather, George Cambridge Urlin, and four other men subdivided the area, sold the lots, named the streets, and called the area Grandview Heights.

George Urlin donated the original plot for the library. Back then it was just a small building on the corner of Ashland and First Avenue. Cambridge Avenue came from his middle name and, naturally, Urlin, his last. He also named Ridgway after his daughter, Marguerite Urlin Ridgway.

He was a man of many business interests. In his obituary they called him an entrepreneur, but I just called him 'Grandpa'."

MARGE FRANCE WHITNEY

Marge France Whitney at her Summit Chase home

"I am energized by watching children learn or see something in a new way."

JENNIFER REED

Mrs. Reed's kindergarten class celebrates Dr. Seuss' birthday

"The Spanish-style, one-floor home has an interior atrium courtyard. All rooms circle the huge double-glass, domed patio. The decor gives the effect of a large outdoor European courtyard surrounded by pillars. The lighting fixtures and hardware are by Tiffany."

"SHELTERING A HERITAGE"

Old Homes of Grandview Heights and Marble Cliff, Ohio

Claudia, Steve, Maggie, Lori and Henry Valachovic in their "Patio Room"

"When we finally got it to work, Jenny and I were both so happy. We were jumping up and down, laughing and clapping our hands."

SARAH SWINFORD

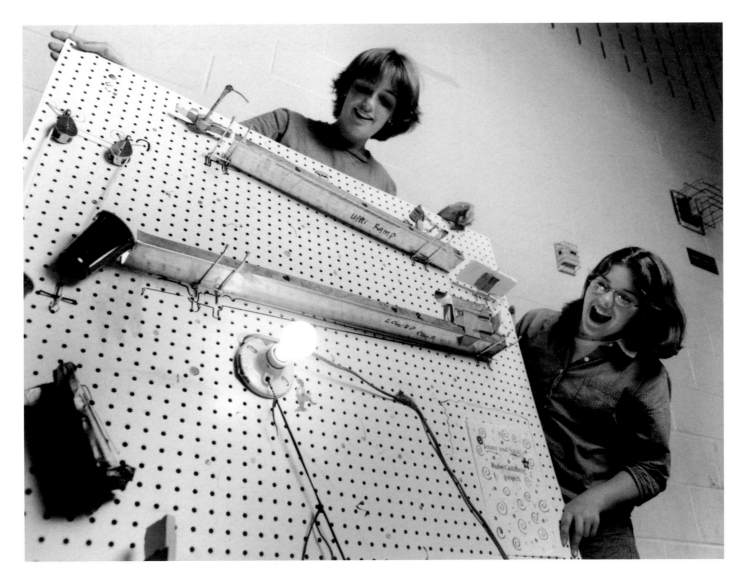

Eighth graders Sarah Swinford and Jenny Rill with their "Rube Goldberg" light switch

"Half a century with a great wife, a great family, a great career,

in a great community."

BILL TYZNIK

Ohio State University Professor Emeritus and inventor Bill Tyznik,
and Bette, his wife and life partner

"The garden - with its pond, water wheel and many plants and buildings - takes up a corner next to the garage. The Hill's started their rail line in 1996. The MacKay comes from Dan's middle name, and the Mills from a previous interest in water-powered mills."

Tiffany Volpe

Tri-Village News

Dan and Katy Hill and their MacKay Mills Railroad

"The Gentile, the Jew, and the Ascension."

Ken Frick

Patty and Mitch Levitt at the Grandview Heights/Marble Cliff Education Foundation Gala at the Columbus Athenaeum

"Our fire department started as a volunteer unit. Old Fire Engine #1 could have been seen roaring out of the municipal building in the 1920s and for many years. Old #1 is now restored and still in running condition."

"Our Proud Heritage" A Coloring Book of Grandview Heights and Marble Cliff History, produced by Edison Elementary School, 2nd edition, 1984

Fire Chief Hank Kauffman and "Truck 1," a 1924 Seagraves

"Following an act by the Ohio Legislature, James Bryden, R.W.

Cowles and John Tipton, Franklin County Commissioners,

purchased a farm owned by Joel Buttles, prominent merchant,

land owner, and banker, and his partner, Mathew Matthews.

The farm was designated for construction as a 'Poor House,'

the first such institution of its kind in Franklin County..."

"Sheltering a Heritage"

Old Homes of Grandview Heights and Marble Cliff, Ohio

Ben, Debbie, Michael, Laura and Zach Brannan's "Poor House"

"The middle school team, made up of seventh-, eighth- and ninth-graders placed eleventh in a field of forty (at the state Science Olympiad contest). The high school team, consisting of sophomores, juniors and seniors, placed fifth in the state in the high school division."

KRISTIN CAMPBELL

Tri-Village News

Middle School Science Olympiad team members and their coaches

"After living here for a few months, we discovered that Marble Cliff, just like Grandview, is a community of friendly, helpful people; a village of charming, interesting homes, each with its own story and appeal."

MARCIA GANTZ

Marcia and Curtis Gantz

"These quotes are honest, poignant and a reminder to pay very close attention to those in the middle - they may push us away, but they still need us to pull and guide and reassure them that they are on the right track to being wonderful and productive 'beings'."

DIANE POWELL

"Messages - To Parents and Teachers," Mrs. Powell's sixth-grade bulletin board

"The Tri-Village Post Office is one of the busiest in the district. Customers often compliment us on being friendly and efficient and we, in turn, feel honored to work in a warm, caring and generous community. We, as a unit, have won several revenue-related awards and most recently an award for selling more Breast Cancer Research stamps than any station in the Columbus Performance Cluster for offices level 18 through 21. We are quite proud of this accomplishment, however, we realize our patrons should receive the approbation."

JOHN H. BALLENTINE

John Ballentine, Window Service Clerk Technician at the Tri-Village Finance Post Office

"The Cake Walk dates back to the time when the event was spectacular and called for formal attire. It's a great way to raise money for the band, as well as a fun social event. The event raised approximately $3000 this year."

DALE MARIE JONES

Cake Walk Chairwoman

The 51st Annual "Cake Walk"

"During Rob and Todd's four years in high school the basketball team went 74-24, were District runners-up twice, went to the 'Elite Eight' and to the state 'Final Four'."

SHERRY LOVEGROVE

Rob Kingston and Todd Lovegrove, GHHS Bobcat basketball co-captains

"Our focus is to reach out into the community and perform for the seniors, local nursing homes and other schools. It's a program that benefits both the community and the kids."

Jim Shaw

Music Director

The Stevenson Singers

37 Kenworth trucks

70 drivers

2000 gallons of diesel fuel each day

937,000 average mileage on each tractor

Each tractor – $80,000

Each trailer – $17,000; $26,000 with a refrigeration unit

Annual mileage – 3.2 million miles

Drivers payroll in October – $349,000, plus $136,000 in benefits

Transportation budget for fiscal 2000 – $6,000,000

WILLIAM NESBITT

Transportation Manager

"It takes a lot of dollars to get you that loaf of bread."

BILL LAWHEAD

Big Bear Stores

The Big Bear Garage

"When we bought this house my husband said he was going to climb that tree!"

Kathy Cosgrove

Mike Cosgrove and his tree

"I know what she's thinking, 'I know the answer, should I raise my hand or not?'"

BOB MEIER, SARAH'S DAD

Sarah Meier, and classmates Maggie Clemens and Emily Bruns,
in Mrs. Strider's first-grade class, Edison Elementary School

"The mark of a good guidance counselor is that they can 'tell it like it is' while, at the same time, be nurturing and supportive. Joe Connors has earned the respect and trust of students, staff and parents because he himself treats everyone with dignity and respect."

PAUL KULIK

Superintendent of Schools

Joe Connors, Teacher of the Year

"To Cole Carnevale,

At last! The moment your father's been waiting for since you were born: the sight of you in a baseball uniform before a cheering crowd. Have a wonderful time.

Love, Mom and Dad"

"To Miguel, Jennifer and Kie,

You guys make a fantastic team. Your dedication to our kids and the hundreds of hours it takes to put on a major league hit like this are deeply appreciated.

Parents of cast, crew and pit."

FROM THE "DAMN YANKEES" PROGRAM

The cast and crew of "Damn Yankees"

"The day was probably the best I've had out of all the days at Edison School."

MY TRIP TO MARS

A Journal entry by Kelsey Kinnard, March 10

"Marsville," the annual Edison Elementary School 5th grade expedition to Mars

"My garden is mostly for me. It is my mental health retreat. It soothes the soul. It gives me time to think through problems while getting some exercise. It is rewarding to see things grow and to witness the constancy of nature's cycles.

I am a teacher at Whitehall-Yearling High School. I love my profession, my subject area, and my students. Students and gardening are very much alike - both need that personal touch to thrive."

SERENA M. BRADSHAW, PH.D. OSU 1977

Serena Bradshaw, gardener and teacher of U.S. History

"We don't meltdown under pressure!"

Sue Godez' "FIRST Team" with their robot "Isys"

"That's the best TP job I've ever seen!"

NEIGHBOR, RITA SCHMALZ

The TP'd house of Phil and Susie Gehrisch

"The Grandview Heights Marble Cliff Historical Society
is dedicated to discover, collect and preserve information,
materials, structures and landmarks which may help to
establish interest in the historic record of the founding and
development of the communities of Grandview Heights and
Marble Cliff. The society has over 150 members."

TRACY LIBERATORE

Grandview Heights Marble Cliff Historical Society

Members of the Grandview Heights Marble Cliff Historical Society

"The middle school raised $1,400 to benefit Operation Feed. That amount will provide 2,800 meals at area food pantries, emergency shelters and soup kitchens."

LIN BENSEN

Family and Consumer Science teacher

"The students here have done just an incredible job and we're so grateful."

JOHN MAY

Director of Operation Feed

Middle School Tug of War for "Operation Feed"

"Most of the boxwoods in Grandview got their start from our yard. Victor Ries, the prior owner of the property, had a sign by the sidewalk stating that the 'garden was open,' inviting everyone to stop by for a clipping to start their own plants. We found the sign in the garage when we bought the place.

Victor, who taught horticulture at Ohio State, planted over 250 varieties of the boxwood on the grounds. Most of them are still here."

TED CELESTE

Bobbie and Ted Celeste and their home of twenty years

Gas Pains

The Clark Station on Fifth Avenue during a mid-June price surge

"The 3200 relay team of Jamie McIntire, Cindy Mattiaccy, Erin Herl and Alli Grace (who also qualified in the 1600 and 3200) qualified for state after finishing with a school record 9:51. Also advancing to state were the boys 3200 relay of Carson Peterson, Rich Bartholomew, Jeff McManus and Jared Lairmore (who also qualified in the 800)."

SHAWN HATEM

This Week in Grandview

Rob Ballinger, varsity track coach

"What I love about track is the excitement. There is excitement in all the events, but my favorite is running hurdles. Hurdles are amazing, but with one wrong step you could end up on the ground and left behind. There is no better feeling in the world than when you are finished with your race, if you ran it the way you wanted to."

MICHAELINE SEXTON

Michaeline Sexton warms up for varsity hurdles

"Each child is involved in an act. They each have a role, everything from being tigers and elephants to being clowns or a magician. We even have a ringmaster."

CAROLYN NYLAND

Retired Stevenson teacher and coordinator of the circus at Edison Elementary

Kiley Landusky and Gretchen Giltner, Kindergarten Circus performers

"I felt we were in a bubble protected from everything and nothing could go wrong. This night belonged to Nathan, myself and our friends."

KRISTIN PARKER

Kristin Parker and Nathan Swift at the Prom

"My family moved to Grandview in the spring of 1930 to a house on Ashland Avenue. My sister just sold that house ending a 70-year period that a Donaldson family member had lived there. The friendly neighborhoods, big trees, good schools, and public library that made our town a desirable place to live and raise a family back then are still the basis of the community's appeal today."

LORNA "SKIP" DONALDSON KARLOVEC

Gene "Tank" and Lorna "Skip" Karlovec

"I'm from the old school. Be fair and live by the Golden Rule."

FRANK MONACO

Frank Monaco, Mayor of Marble Cliff, Ohio

"We were confident and thick in talent, more so than the other teams I played on. Although young, we knew we had the skills and brains to outplay any team on any given day."

NICK ERVIN

Class of 2000

The Bobcat Battery

"Best of Show"

Lee "Doc" Ekleberry

Art Instructor

Joshua Santilli, Class of 2000, at the annual GHHS Art Show

"After lying vacant for several years in the early 1940s, part of the land was designated as the Victory Gardens, where many residents grew food as a way to support the World War II effort locally by raising crops to can and eat."

LORNA "SKIP" KARLOVEC

Grandview Heights Marble Cliff Historical Society

Prayin' for rain at the Wallace Gardens

"Trinity United Methodist Church celebrates with the new confirmands and their families as the students become full members of the church. Throughout the class, students learn about their heritage, the uniqueness of being United Methodist, and the importance of a relationship with God through Jesus Christ."

ERIC HAGELY

Director of High School and Youth Adult Ministries

Confirmation Class, Trinity United Methodist Church

The dress Caroline is wearing belonged to her great, great grandmother Elizabeth Dixon, Mary Todd Lincoln's friend and comforter at Abraham Lincoln's deathbed.

The booties worn by Lizzy in the photograph were presented to her great, great, great grandmother by Red Cloud, Chief of the Oglala Sioux.

Caroline and daughter, Elizabeth Dixon Van Deusen

"The highlight of my career was when my daughter, Amy, came into business with me. She is now ready to spread her wings. On December 28, I leave for the Big Island and begin my new life there. Aloha."

JENNI LONG

Amy Berry and Jenni Long of the Tri-Village Studio

"McCain's bus is on its way back to Ohio."

SAM DONALDSON OF ABC NEWS

Presidential candidate John McCain's "Straight Talk Express" at Custom Coach

"By far the most personally satisfying function to date in my term of office has been handing out the diplomas to our graduating seniors. At the risk of sounding trite, I felt that day that I was shaking hands with unparalleled opportunity and looking directly into the eyes of tremendous promise for the future."

SUZANNE MCLEOD

President, Grandview Heights Board of Education

School Board members Ron Cameron, Kathy Lithgow, Brian Cook,

Suzanne McLeod and Steve Burigana

"The St. Christopher's Festival was a church tradition in the 1950s and that's what we hope it will be again. The 2000 Festival was the first in many years and for our first year back we felt it was very successful. It raised funds for general parish improvements."

MARIE FLYNN

2000 Chairwoman

Keirstin Bragg at the St. Christopher's Festival

"I wish the whole world was like my town, happy, healthy, close, most of all. We genuinely care for each other."

TESSA MEDERSKI

Tessa Mederski

"Integrity Painting is privileged to be a part in maintaining the heritage and character of the homes and the community of Grandview Heights and Marble Cliff."

DALE JAGGER

Integrity Painting, Ltd.

Employees of Integrity Painting at the home of Leah Houser and Mark Woodhouse

"It was a hot, blustery afternoon as we pulled into the parking lot of Our Lady of Victory Church. Outside, parents were busy taking pictures of all the children who looked like little brides and grooms. I'll always remember how proud and excited we were that day. Not only because it was Taylor's first communion, but also because it was the first class of the new millennium. There really was something special about this first class, just as all of the other firsts of this year have been special. And as time passes, memories from this year will probably always burn just a little brighter."

JEFF PICKERING

Taylor Pickering, with parents Jeff and Robin at her First Communion,
Our Lady of Victory Church

"The people at Boulevard Presbyterian Church need a cow."

Bob Connors

610 WTVN Radio

"The Children of Boulevard Presbyterian Church have really embraced the idea of helping others through their involvement in a global charity organization. The children, ages 3 to 11, have given their weekly offerings to support Heifer Project International. HPI's mission is to promote self-sufficiency by providing farm animals to families in need."

MICHELLE WILSON

Stewardship Representative

"This Sunday we celebrate our donation of a heifer cow to a village in Honduras."

LAURIE WARD

Director of Children's Ministries

Lana the Jersey Cow at Boulevard Presbyterian Church

"Seven children, three of the best dogs in the world, one supremely independent feline and four plastic fish... We have a rather unique family! Add that to the fact we have had the privilege of being Grandview residents for 25 years. We are truly blessed with a marvelous combination of family, friends and community!

All seven of our children have been foreign exchange students: Sayaka from Japan, Pekka from Finland, Neil from Argentina, Manuel "Menu" from Switzerland, Maude from France, and Soeren and Michael from Germany. It has been an incredibly rewarding adventure. Love is a gift you give others and often get in return. We have friends and family on four continents who open their doors and arms to us as we travel."

ASONYA MCKINNEY BROWN

Asonya Brown, foreign exchange student Soeren Schroeder, and city attorney

Gary Brown, two days before Soeren's return home to Germany

"It is my muse, my collaborator in the endless process of artistic development. It gives voice to the faint mumblings of my soul; I rise to the challenge it presents."

PAUL BURKEY

Grandview's first Martin Essex Scholar

Paul Burkey and his bass

"I believe when a district like Grandview performs well it's a credit to the quality of the teachers and a credit to parents, who are the primary educators. Education is truly a partnership. We need to rely on parents and teachers sharing that responsibility. Fortunately, in Grandview, we have that partnership."

PAUL KULIK

Dr. Paul E. Kulik, Superintendent of Schools

Traditionally scheduled on Thursday evening of the Memorial Day weekend, the Grandview Heights service is always the first in Franklin County. It is sponsored by the Blue Star Mothers - Tri-Village Unit, and the City of Grandview Heights.

VFW Hilliard Post #614 members at the Grandview Heights Memorial Service

"Mortally wounded by small arms fire and dies on battlefield,
Kien Hao Province. February 25, 1969."

Excerpt from the biography of: Titus, James Elroy, in
"A History of the Redfox-Sparling and Related Families"
447 pages, copyright 1975 Elroy W. Titus

The American Gold Star Mothers was formed over 70 years
ago to honor the sons and daughters lost in time of war.
Mrs. Titus is the local chapter president. She still displays
the Gold Star symbol in her front window.

Laura C. Titus - Gold Star Mother with the framed medals earned by husband Elroy in WWII and Korea, and son Jimmy in Vietnam

"At the risk of his own life, (Hartwell) crawled forward to the wounded men and although under continuous heavy fire, succeeded in carrying to safety the company commander and two enlisted men."

U.S. Army Press Center

February, 1945

John Hartwell, World War II veteran,
Grand Marshal of the Memorial Day Parade, and golfer

"Getting third place was very special for my very first competitive Soap Box Derby race in my whole life."

BETHANY ANDERSON

Bethany Anderson, 9, goes "heels over head" for the Soap Box Derby

"The Fab Five"

CYNTHIA MCKAY

Cynthia McKay, Susan Van Ausdale, Melissa Marcus,
John McElheny and Nora Durham with their Beetles

"They'll be dancing in the streets of Marble Cliff."

Jeff Link

Tri-Village News

GRANDVIEW HEIGHTS 114 MARBLE CLIFF, OHIO

The Lajkonic Polish Folk Dancers at Paul J. Falco Park, performing for the

Village's Music in the Park series

"I could tell they'd been here!"

ANONYMOUS

Bank Block Elephant Walk

"What wonderful faces. And hardly a full set of front teeth among them!"

SUSAN AZZANO-KUKLA

The Braves and Reds T-ball teams

"The mid-west's best 80's band, The Reaganomics, are a group of musicians specializing in eighties rock. Not to be confused with a controversial economic theory, The Reaganomics are dedicated to bringing back the statement and feeling that defined music in the previous decade."

"THE REAGANOMICS" WEB PAGE

"The Reaganomics" perform for the "Music on the Lawn" series at the
Grandview Heights Public Library

"My husband, John, was born in Grandview and I lived there until I entered the first grade. Now we do everything there. Both of us love it. Our parish, St. Christopher, is there. We have friends and a lot of family there."

RACHAEL ABBRUZZESE

Rachael and Johnny Abbruzzese, loving "The Reaganomics"

"Cyclists from 14 countries are competing for a total purse of $28,000, with $14,000 in prize money awarded in each of the men's and women's divisions. Ten cyclists who will be competing in the 2000 Summer Olympics in Australia are among the competitors."

TRICIA SYMANSIC

This Week in Grandview

The Wendy's International Racing Classic

"Rested and ready for what the road brings. Twenty-four members of Boulevard Presbyterian Church's Youth Group embark on a 618-mile journey to a work camp in Kinston, NC. There they will join hundreds of other campers to repair the devastation caused a year earlier by hurricane Floyd. After a week's labor in the hot, humid weather of North Carolina, neither the town of Kinston nor these twenty-four will ever be the same."

ED WARD

The Youth Ministry Team from Boulevard Presbyterian Church

"July 16 was one of those special days. Cruz had already won the Ohio boys, 13 years old and under, 800 meter championship, and the win this day at the regionals in Lexington, KY, qualified him for the National Junior Olympic Track Meet in Buffalo, NY. There he would go on to finish 22nd in the nation.

This was also the day of the Little League championship game where my Yankees were to play the Grant Douglass, Bryan Davis-coached Phillies. During the season Spencer had played all over the field, but this day had chosen to cheer for his older brother. Les Viragh coached in my absence, and in an exciting game with excellent play by both teams, pulled out a 2-1 victory for the championship."

BRUCE DAVIS

Brothers Cruz and Spencer Davis

"... the fuzzy slippers that my best friend and I bought together, the cowboy hat 'I had to have,' my favorite painting, my obsession with glow-in-the-dark stars, all my 11 years of swimming piled into a heap of trophies, plaques, medals and ribbons...."

AMY WILLIAMS, ON "HER ROOM"

Amy Williams

"It was the best weather we've had in seven years."

JERI DIEHL-CUSACK

Director, Grandview Heights Public Library

Samantha Eggers, Christi Gehrisch and Lauren Colley perform at "Lazy Days,"
the annual library and City of Grandview Heights fund raiser

"I've always believed that creativity is more important than knowledge...

The creative energy of children is contagious...

The pursuit of creativity is a lifelong endeavor..."

KATHY GRACE

Kathy Grace in her studio

"We also offer ourselves, as ones who take them into our love,

our prayers, and our daily lives, striving, for their nurturing,

to build in this place a community rich in the Spirit of God."

July 9th bulletin, First Community Church

The Baptism of Connor Michael McNary

"Iggy Ba Diggy, Wiggy

Uff Uff - A duffa wuffa

Go Gators Go!"

The "Gator" cheer

Alex Minnillo and Joey Stewart of the Grandview Gator Swim Team

"Ron puts up the flags and bunting for Memorial Day, but the kids and grandchildren love it so much that it usually stays up until the snow flies."

Jo Ann Curry

Ron and Jo Ann Curry with grandchildren Carley and Cassidy Rowe

"Lauren and I are totally in love with N'SYNC and would do ANYTHING, I do mean anything, to meet them. The radio contest was this: paint your garage with N'SYNC, the station, and the morning show, and we had a chance for two backstage passes and front row seats."

ANNIE MARUKHLENKO

"I rode by the garage and saw the two of them etching something on the garage door. I knew that either they had gone wacko or there was some kind of a boy band contest. From then on, I was officially the paint boy. I really liked it."

JOHN MYERS

"When I heard that we didn't win the contest I was devastated: Annie was also. There weren't very good tickets for the show in Columbus so we bought tickets for the Cleveland show. We had a great time and will never forget the experience."

LAUREN STYER

Annie Marukhlenko, John Myers and Lauren Styer and their WNCI entry

for back stage passes to an N'SYNC concert

"St. Raphael's opened in February 1948, operating out of the former home of Samuel Prescott Bush, grandfather of former President George Bush. A three-story expansion to the original building was opened in 1950, expanding St. Raphael's capacity from 15 to 78.

St. Raphael's Home for the Aged is making plans to move its operations out of Marble Cliff to a new building at the Villas of St. Therese on East Broad Street."

Alan Froman

This Week in Grandview

In the days of his youth, future president George Bush slid down this banister.

Urban Legend

The Carmelite Sisters for the Aged and Infirm

"A wish for one carousel horse has led to twenty years of collecting, increasing our knowledge and artistic awareness of carousel art, and the meeting of delightful new friends."

SALLY KOSNIK

The "Corn Maiden," "Millie" the ostrich, and a horse with no name, with Sally Kosnik

Rec Center Fever!

Don Hamilton and the Grandview Jolly Steppers

"The Ox Roast starts off the school year, always the weekend after Labor Day, and a lot of people come back into town for it. It serves as a reunion.

The roast raises about $20,000 and all of that money goes to students in the school district."

RAY DeGRAW

Bobcat Boosters Publicity Chairman

Jessica Walton and Kristen Polomik (in seat 3)
on the "King Swing" at the Ox Roast

"I ran at Sebring, Daytona, Watkins Glen, Road America,

Indianapolis and Le Mans. When I was with Carroll Shelby

back in '65 we were world champions. We had Mario Andretti,

Dave McDonald, Dan Gurney, Phil Hill, Ed Leslie, Jo Schlesser,

Bob Bondurant and Ken Miles on that team. I was also six-time

national champion."

BOB JOHNSON

Bob Johnson, race car driver and caterer

"60,000 haircuts, that would be my guess."

Dennis Hammond, answering the question of how many haircuts he's given in his 21 years in the Grandview area

Dennis Hammond, barber, Men First Hair Design

"When I was a kid I was always playing in my granddad's shop.

I would take naps in the old clawfoot tubs he had on display

in the showroom. And when I got into trouble I'd hide in the

bins that stretched from the floor all the way to the ceiling.

But when I came down my dad would tan my hide.

Granddad opened his shop in 1908 in the area where the

Seville Apartments are now located. Dad moved the business

to our Fifth Avenue location right about 1960."

KEVIN P. GLASS

Kevin P. Glass of Glass Plumbing, Inc., Grandview's longest-operating business

"I am looking forward my dear, with a great deal of pleasure when in the spring we shall be one. To share each others joy or sorrow, as it shall come to us. And looking on the bright side hope that our lives shall be full of joy and happiness. I will do all I possibly can, and I know you will, to make the pathway one of sunshine."

FROM A LOVE LETTER BY GILBERT WITHYCOMBE TO MABEL WILLIAMS, GREAT GRANDPARENTS OF THE BRIDE. WRITTEN JUST PRIOR TO THEIR WEDDING, 1902.

The wedding of Ellen Kindle and Mike Kendall, September 3, Trinity United Methodist Church

"When serving as president of city council I was involved with the purchase of the private swimming pool on Goodale Boulevard for the city and the renovation of the building, replacement of the pool, apron and installing a baby pool. Success with this, and other projects, encouraged me to work toward procuring the property on Goodale Boulevard for a city park. It was the only vacant land in Grandview large enough for a usable park.

After many years of frustration the Ohio Department of Natural Resources made grant money available for the purchase of parkland. A great job was done by many to show the need for the park and grant money was approved."

C. Ray Buck

Ray and Eleanor Buck at the C. Ray Buck Sports Park

"Mom is always telling us 'When I was your age...' stories. One of her favorites is that she and her friends could all stand on their heads. Mom was really excited when she married dad, she found out that he could stand on his head, too. Mom and dad taught the rest of us 'the act' when we were little. We're the only family we know that can all stand on our heads."

ALLY HEYDINGER, AGE 11

Ally, Gary, Renee, Will and Grant Heydinger stand tall

"The Instrumental Music Department at Grandview Heights High School has enjoyed many years of successful performance. Students have several opportunities to perform in a variety of venues during their high school music experience, including the Marching Band, Concert Band, Pep Band, and are given the opportunity to audition for the Jazz Ensemble and perform in the pit orchestra for the annual musical production."

KIE WATKINS

Band Director, middle and high schools

The Grandview Heights High School Marching Band tuba section

"The staff of Robert Louis Stevenson Elementary believes that all children have the power to learn and achieve their highest academic and social potential. The staff, children, parents, and community are responsible for working together to develop globally aware, life-long learners by building strong self-esteems and providing a secure environment."

ROBERT LOUIS STEVENSON MISSION STATEMENT

Cheryl Hilton, Robert Louis Stevenson Elementary School principal
with the school's prized scrapbook dating back to the 1920's

"Older adults with developmental disabilities from the Senior Additional Growth Experiences (SAGE) program at Goodwill Columbus thoroughly enjoy their intergenerational experiences with eighth graders from Grandview Heights Middle School. Such activities provide a tremendous opportunity for both generations to learn from each other and to develop relationships that are cherished by all involved."

CAROL D. FARMER, M.S.

Director, Senior Services

SAGE Program participant George Dalton plays Bingo with 8th graders Rachel Cropper and Val Elliot

"When I was about 14 I got interested in cars and girls. I took a saber saw and cut my railroad platform into manageable sections and hauled it to the curb. I called it the 'Great Grandview Train Massacre.'

I've spent thirty years of my life getting it back."

BILL ANTHONY

Bill Anthony, owner of Buki's Toys and Trains

"I love this street!"

Tom Roberts

Tom Roberts of McClain Road

"He is incredibly tuned-in to children and into making music fun. Many music teachers are more concerned about content. Jim focuses on the child and on having a good time, not so much on developing a perfect voice or playing an instrument perfectly."

CHERYL HILTON

Principal, Robert Louis Stevenson Elementary School

Jim Shaw, elementary music teacher

Paul J. Falco

1915-1996

"In 1954, Paul became a member of the Marble Cliff Village
Council and served six years before becoming mayor in 1960.
Paul was Mayor of Marble Cliff for 36 years - one of the
longest serving mayors in the nation. Paul drove around the
Village daily, checking traffic lights, streets, trees, and trash
removal. As mayor he successfully promoted business and
commercial development of the Village."

INSCRIPTION ON THE MEMORIAL IN FALCO PARK

Marble Cliff Village Council members in the Paul J. Falco Park

"Grandview is the best place to raise a family. It was the love of our town and the appreciation of what we have enjoyed over the years here that inspired me to run for mayor. It was also out of concern that as we approach a major period of growth and change, that the delicate balance between our residents and business community be protected."

N. COLLEEN SEXTON

Colleen Sexton, Mayor of Grandview Heights, Ohio

"Grandview Heights embraces all the amenities of the 'big' city with an exceptional quality of life only found in small hometowns. Its businesses and residents enjoy tree-lined streets, excellent schools and state-of-the-art library. Known for its city services, the City of Grandview Heights is a safe community where policemen are neighbors and fire and emergency medical services react in just two minutes."

GRANDVIEW HEIGHTS WEB PAGE

Grandview Heights City Council

"The Bobcats took the opening kickoff and capped a 66-yard drive with a one-yard run by sophomore running back Alex Picazo. Picazo carried four times for 43 yards and a touchdown on the opening drive, and finished with 132 yards on 25 carries to become the first Bobcat to break the 100-yard barrier this season."

CHRIS HOGAN

This Week in Grandview

Bobcat "Homecoming Dance"

"We fell in love with our cottage on a sunny May day when the yard was full of blooming daffodils. We knew little about its history. As people did knock on our door we gradually learned more. One visitor was the daughter of the architect, Paul Tibbals. Mr. Tibbals, we are told, built 5 or so homes around this corner of Mulford, Woodhill and Bluff and named the subdivision Utopia. All the homes were built around 1939, at a time when the land south of Bluff was a forest."

FRAN BALCH

Fran Balch and her home on Woodhill Drive

Badger, at 17 pounds, the true Big Cat in Grandview; Abigail,

at an estimated 137 BPM (barks per minute), the barkingest

dog in town.

Badger the cat and Abigail the Miniature Schnauzer
held by owners Bill and Sue Riesenberger

"The Grandview Heights Public Library's Governing Board is made up of seven community members who are appointed by the Board of Education.

These seven Trustees set the policies and guidelines under which the staff operates on a daily basis. They stand as overseers of legal compliance to all State and Federal laws and regulations."

GRANDVIEW HEIGHTS PUBLIC LIBRARY

Grandview Heights Public Library Board of Trustees

"Chef Hubert Seifert continues to roll with the punches in giving customers what they want. From 1981 to the present his eclectic, upbeat, yet comfortable restaurant remains a catalyst in the Grandview area. Be sure to watch for the chef in the dining room as he enjoys strong interaction with his customers."

NICOLE SEIFERT

Chef Hubert Seifert of SPAGIO

Krema, number one in nuts!

The Krema Nut Company, the oldest continually operating nut company in America

"Catalpa trees line Roxbury Road providing shade, beauty and the feel of a country lane. Their canopy of broad leaves, white flowers, and bean-like seedpods induce an inviting feel for our Frank Packard 19th century "Swiss-style, summer cottage." Neighbors take time to visit with each other during the annual spring Catalpa bean rake up. Our stately Catalpas signify comfort and community - they are one of our village treasures."

THE STUDEBAKERS

Susan, Colin, Kent and Aaron Studebaker

"Ahh, me and my babies!"

CHRIS MARSHALL

Restaurateur Chris Marshall, Brutus, and the Harley

"The Bank Block building was forecasted in a July 1928 issue of 'The Community News' to include 'mammoth' parking capacity for 350 cars, 'with painted signs by day and neon lighted signs by night,' as well as a 'uniformed attendant with special police powers insuring the safety of cars, bundles, and children who may be left under his care'."

Jeff Link

Tri-Village News

"When we first bought the building the city wanted us to tear it down."

Mike Wagenbrenner

Mike and Tom Wagenbrenner, developers of the Bank Block

"People are now in the open about death – they're not so opposed to talking about it. Today we talk to schoolchildren about death. Children don't have to dwell on death but they need to know that these are the things that are real in life."

IVAN DAVIS

Ivan and Jeff Davis of the Deyo-Davis Funeral Home

"D.A.R.E. - Drug Abuse Resistance Education - is a preventative program originally developed in Los Angeles. Uniformed law enforcement officers teach the curriculum in schools, aiming to equip young people with skills to resist peer pressure to experiment with harmful drugs. The concept is straightforward and simple - D.A.R.E. to say 'NO!'"

D.A.R.E. LITERATURE

Officer Michael Small of the D.A.R.E. Program with role models
Austin Carter and Jill Elder speaking to Mrs. Fiumera's 5th graders

"Bill bought his first day lilies in 1990 and joined the local day lily club a year later. We've added sculptures and an Italian fountain. We are now an official American Hemercallus Display Garden and grow over 500 different cultivars."

GAIL TYLER JOHANNES

Gail and Bill Johannes

HATS OFF ...

HATS ARE OUR SYMBOL

IN THE LIGHT OR THE DARK

ONE ALWAYS RECOGNIZES US BY

OUR SPECIAL MARK

WE ARE SEEN FOR MILES AWAY

OUR HATS NEVER SWAY

THEY BRIGHTEN OUR DAY

FROM A POEM BY SISTER MICHELLE MOORE

Activity Director, St. Raphael's Home for the Aged

Mrs. Albina Marson, St. Raphael's Home For the Aged

"On Halloween night me and my friend Mario went down Glenn Avenue and Mulford Road. We were clowns for Halloween. The clown shoes we wore were very hard to walk in. I won first place in the Halloween Festival. My favorite candy is PAY DAY bars."

ROBERT MAUPIN

Robert Maupin, 8, and Mario Fortin, 9, "trick or treat" on Mulford Road

"What is art to me? Art stands as the freest form of communication. It is using a medium to express more than what it physically is. Art should hold an idea that can be taken in as many ways as possible, to fit the individual. The less direct the message, the more complicated a piece of art can become."

COLE CARNEVALE

Cole Carnevale, painting a mural in the Stevenson Elementary School library

"Pals Forever" and "Friends Always"

INDIAN GUIDES AND INDIAN PRINCESSES SLOGANS

Indian Guides and Indian Princesses in Wyman Woods

"Four seconds to play, down by two, Kevin shoots for tree!"

Ken Frick

Kevin Frick plays "one on one"

"With the talent and maturity of this year's girls basketball squad, the Bobcats are hoping to bring back some winning spirit of yore.

'Grandview girls basketball has been very successful through the years,' Bobcats coach Steve Hall said. 'One of the things we've been trying to do is carry on the tradition that the program has had in the past'."

BRADLEY EIMER
Tri-Village News

The 2000-2001 GHHS Girls Varsity Basketball Team

"To tell you the truth, I would be surprised and even disappointed if we didn't succeed this year. We have potential but we have to prove it and that is by how hard the kids are willing to work.

The team is a pretty close-knit group. They are all hard workers and, when they are in a battle, they pick each other up, which is always good."

COACH ANDY DiSABATO

The Grandview Heights High School Varsity Wrestling team

"St. Christopher has had bingo since 1960 when its profits went to paying off the church and rectory debt. Bingo has been used in the past thirty years to pay for air conditioning in the Bingo hall, and reduction of tuition for students attending Catholic grade school, as well as some help for families that have children in Catholic high schools."

JOHN DAWSON

St. Christopher Church

"I'm told we have the best Bingo food in town."

DENIS BLAKE

Kitchen manager

Friday night Bingo at St. Christopher Church

"The Birthday Book Wall is a collection of bookplates acknowledging gifts of books to the Trinity Elementary School Library from students celebrating a birthday.

The birthday students are proud to share their books with the class. They are the first to check out the book and take it home to share with their families. These 'Special Collection' books will remain in the library for many years and will be enjoyed by many children."

JANE BREHL

Librarian, Trinity Elementary School

The Birthday Books at Trinity Elementary School

"Anita Elking, Michelle Norris (who ran for the injured Pam McManus) and Karen Riggs hoped to raise $500 for the Grandview Heights/Marble Cliff Education Foundation by running in the October 29 Columbus Marathon. The trio ran as a relay team, wearing T-shirts that read 'Grandview Gala Gals.' The team raised more than $700 and completed the 26.2 mile course in about four hours."

KRISTIN CAMPBELL

Tri-Village News

*"Grandview Gala Gals" Pam McManus, Karen Riggs, Anita Elking
and Michelle Norris*

"The secret to living long but staying young, loving fully
and laughing heartily; be happy - *BALLROOM DANCE!*"

DANCE PLUS

Mary Kovach and Scott Roberts at Dance Plus

"At AEP training and safety go hand-in-hand. Well-trained employees see safety as the main tool used to perform their job. The returns from a job performed by a well-trained, safety-minded crew show up in profit, worker satisfaction, public safety and worker confidence. This says it all, 'No operating condition or urgency of service can ever justify endangering the life of anyone'."

DOUGLAS M. CLEMONS

Training coordinator

American Electric Power

Central Region

Shop mechanics - AEP Station Central Repair Shop

"Grandview Heights is a community connected by sidewalks, which we use every day of the year, rain, snow, or shine. Ever since we rescued our greyhounds through Greyhound Adoption of Ohio, we have been walking them all over town and falling in love with the people, homes, and restaurants that make Grandview Heights our special 'small town.' This coming spring, 2001, we'll be adding a stroller alongside the dogs with the birth of our first child!"

DAVID AND JEAN CULBERTSON

"We have prayers of joy to share this morning, because we have a new baby here at Boulevard. Garrett Charles Culbertson, Dave and Jean Culbertson's little boy was born yesterday on the 23rd at 10:15 A.M. Jean and Garrett expect to be coming home tomorrow on Christmas Day."

THE REVEREND JANICE HILKERBAUMER
Boulevard Presbyterian Church

Jean and David Culbertson with greyhounds Willow and Mulder

"Grandview is just an excellent place to work. The city really takes care of us. Once you hire on here you generally stay until retirement. People don't often see the fire or police, but we're at their homes every week. We get a lot of letters and calls from people complimenting our crews."

GARY BROWNING

Service Department Supervisor

"During the year 2000 the Service Department collected 3,729.21 tons of refuse, 141.25 tons of recyclables, and an estimated 400 tons of newspapers and magazines."

SAM TROIANO

Director of Services

Ken Geddie of the Street Department

"We do it because of the kids. We started building our collection

when I was in the Army. We've picked up things in Texas,

Tennessee, Frankenmuth, Michigan and Nashville in Indiana.

Our first year here was in 1993 and the display has changed

every year. It takes maybe three days to do the outside and two

more for the inside. But it's worth it to watch the kids' faces."

CLAYTON MILLER

Linda and Clayton Miller's home on Second Avenue

"My front door has a greeting of 'I Love Winter.' Once you walk in you realize I'm not kidding. I used to hate how bare the house would look the 2nd week of January after Christmas decorations were put away. Now snowmen fill the house clear through 'til the last snow of the season. My husband calls them my winter decor!"

DENISE LARSON

Newlyweds Denise and Sven Larson and the "snowmen"

"My friends and I hung out a lot over winter break. Our favorite places to talk and eat were Stauf's, Mon Aimee, and Bruegger's Bagels. Sometimes we would find ourselves in the middle of the conversations about the weirdest things, and wonder 'How did we get here?!'"

KATHY WARD

7th grade

Sled riders Chloe Hammond, Molly McCloskey and Kathy Ward

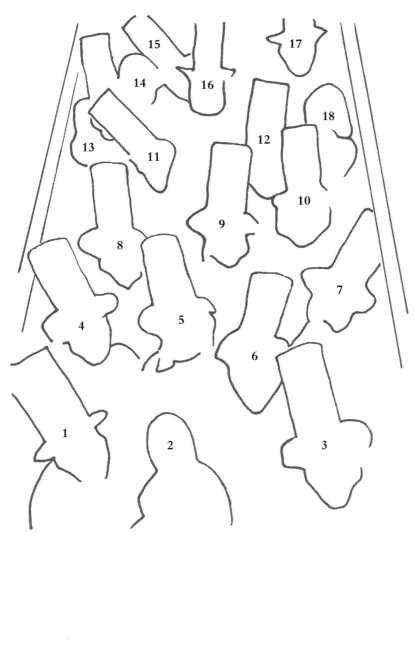

Dr. Seuss' birthday – Page 5
1. Danny Morrill
2. Josh Daugherty
3. Aaron Thomas
4. Jacob Smith
5. Kathleen Griffith
6. Ryan Grasha
7. Emma Walters
8. Brandon Long
9. Danielle Scott
10. Leila Manirochana
11. Tony Etter
12. Selby Gage
13. Zach Van Gastle
14. Fletcher Bosca
15. Kyleah Burton-Smiles
16. Kelly McPeak
17. Kyle McLain
18. Kelsey Senter

Middle School Science Olympiad Team – Page 21
1. Corban Kell
2. Evan Moore
3. Michael Luczyk
4. Colin Studebaker
5. Jacob Brown
6. Ben Grasha
7. Elizabeth Yerian
8. Mindy Stoltz
9. Craig McMurry
10. Mimi Brown
11. J Hoerath
12. Ben Hartenstein
13. Eric Eickholt
14. Dana Short
15. Nick Gladman
16. Richard Cotterman
17. Leslie Leutz
18. John Leutz
19. Jim Buxton
20. Scott Kell

Stevenson Singers – Page 33
1. Miranda Hannah
2. Faith Gingrich
3. Jennifer Griffith
4. Bailey Lytle
5. Chelsea Farabee
6. Kristen Perry
7. Noah Reed
8. Doug Neff
9. Theresa Albon
10. Holly Cloward
11. Tiffani Cook
12. Jessica Stukey
13. Lucy Thornton-Wourms
14. Chelsea Snell
15. Crosby Franklin
16. Caiti Fisher
17. Maggie McKnight
18. Dan McGraw
19. Ali Kientz

Big Bear Garage – Page 35
1. Clayton Bradshaw
2. Steve Ford
3. Jim Gavorcik
4. Joe Paul
5. John Risch
6. George Terry
7. Dewey Dawson
8. J.T. Snyder
9. Wayne Miller
10. Mike VanGundy
11. Michael A. Caldwell
12. Bruce Willmore

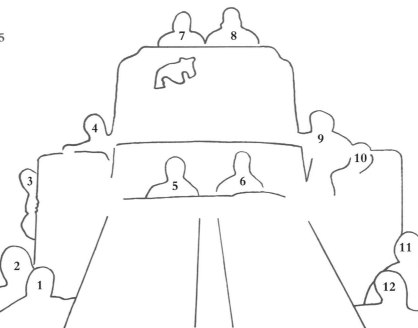

1. Jeff Grunewald
2. Jessica Agler
3. Lauren Colley
4. Jennifer Griffith
5. Miguel Perez
6. Wes Larkin
7. Kate Sutter
8. Jayme Kemmerer
9. Leslie Graves
10. Kara Kaufman
11. Ryan Griggs
12. Nikki Foley
13. Jacqi Szabo
14. Josh Arnold
15. Sarah Grabenstatter
16. Tim Carlson
17. Jason Lange
18. Christi Gehrisch
19. Cole Carnevale
20. Joe Delphia
21. Janese Bovinet
22. Erin Herl
23. Hannah Schwarz
24. Ed Hallam
25. Nick Delphia
26. Ben DeMaria
27. Michaeline Sexton
28. Emily Giglierano
29. Kerry Brumfield
30. Cory Davenport
31. Ben Leither
32. Pete Fusco
33. Art Friscoe
34. Travis Speakman
35. Josh Santilli
36. Joe Shafer
37. Ashleigh Alexander
38. Andrea Leutz
39. Melissa Graves
40. Andie Hardy
41. Kathryn Anstaett

"FIRST" Team – Page 49

1. Erica Abbot
2. Sara Childs
3. Melissa Marcus
4. Sarah Weese
5. Amanda Justice
6. Liz Celeste
7. Nick Ervin
8. Allie Sakas
9. Jordan Gladman
10. Sue Godez
11. Mark Budde
12. Jena Alexander
13. Katie Harvey
14. Rachel Brown
15. Kris Mehling
16. Soeren Schroeder
17. Erin Morris
18. Sarah Ross

Not pictured: Matt DeGraw, Andy Sisinger and Colleen O'Neil

Historical Society – Page 53

1. Tom DeMaria
2. Margie Wilson
3. Win Keller
4. Skip Karlovec
5. Bill Koch
6. Sally Kosnik
7. Jo Ann Curry
8. Pat Mooney
9. Wayne Carlson
10. Tracy Liberatore

Not pictured: Ruthanne James

Tug of War *(left to right)* **– Page 55**
Nathan Osterman
Vince Graves
Craig Cataline
David Murray
Barb Dahmke

Bobcat Battery – Page 73
Shaun Andrews, *front*
Nick Ervin
Jon Grabenstatter
Mike Patterson
Nick Barte
Chase Cordial
Ryan Ranbom

Confirmation Class – Page 79
1. Heather Perry
2. Elizabeth Dangel
3. Elizabeth Yerian
4. C.J. Ford
5. Maggie Mattmiller
6. Lauren Meeth
7. Allison Kuehn
8. Caroline Hoyle
9. Eric Hagely
10. Allie Cassell
11. Hadley Hatch
12. Celeste Savage
13. Christen Zimmerman
14. Laura Vaughn
15. Jen Robenalt
16. Grace Miller
17. Josh Vance
18. Ben Kuhar
19. Tom Casasanta
20. Matt Voelker
21. Matt Inbusch
22. David Boylan
23. Andrew Leininger
24. Rick Thompson
25. Jeffrey Pritchett

Heifer Project *(left to right)* **- Page 97**
Rosie Plas
Emma Swinford
Sarah Swinford
Lana the cow
Chad Davis
Michelle Wilson
Zach Wilson
Marie Fleming - Lana's owner
Connor Wilson

VFW Hilliard Post #614 *(left to right)* **- Page 105**
Steve Erdy-Post 3rd Vice Commander
L. Jack Borowski-Post Adjutant
Arthur Mercier-Post Commander
Donald Warren-Past Commander
John Alther

The Braves and Reds - Page 119
1. Kiley Landusky
2. Brendan Cox
3. Connor Sarich
4. Danny Morrill
5. Tyler Wernet
6. Alex Cochran
7. Aileen Evans
8. Nick Durham
9. Courtney O'Mara
10. Will Heydinger
11. Joe Higgins
12. Andy McCauley
13. Joe Treasure
14. Zachary Nelson
15. Eric Umbarger
16. Hayden Wernet
17. Carter Jump
18. Sean Oberschlake
19. Kyle Priest
20. Jonathan Browning
21. Trevor Voelker
22. Andy Treasure
23. Mechele Gebke
24. Amy Duncan

The Baptism of Connor Michael McNary *(left to right)* - Page 137
Alan Seffens
Pamela Heuer
The Reverend James M. Long
Connor held by Michael McNary
Elsie Dunnington
Nicolette McNary

The Curry's and Rowe's *(left to right)* - Page 141
Carley Rowe
Ron Curry
Cassidy Rowe
Jo Ann Curry
Roni Rowe
Phil Rowe *(back to camera on left)*

The Carmelite Sisters for the Aged and Infirm - Page 145
Bottom to top:
Sister Ann Brown
Sister Michelle Moore
Sister Ann Daily
Sister Kathleen Dominick
Sister Mary Rose Heery
Sister Jacqueline Wagner
Sister Kevin Lynch
Sister Shawn Flynn

The GHHS tuba section *(bottom row, left to right)* - Page 165
Rosie Plas
Brittny Parsons
Megan Gish
　(top row)
David Rill
Anne Nichols
Jeff Bernhard
Jonathon Rohrer

Youth Ministry Mission - Page 127
1. Meredith Porter
2. Holly Henry
3. Megan Porter
4. Rachel Swift
5. Bryn Mandl
6. Missy Truck
7. Justin Birchard
8. Laura Harvey
9. Emily Swift
10. Jared Bovinet
11. Karl Anderson
12. Mike Gillis
13. Tom Stumpp
14. Kelly Waldon
15. Becca Swift
16. Alexandra Gee
17. Sarah Harvey
18. Vicki Rush
19. Ben Ayers
20. Nathan Swift
21. Jeff Reynolds
22. Amy Herkins
23. Robin Reynolds
24. Ed Ward

Marble Cliff Council Members *(left to right)* - **Page 177**

Kent Studebaker
David Roark
Anne Jewel
Jeff King, *top*
Curtis Gantz
Lynda Murray

Grandview Heights City Council - **Page 181**

Kelley A. Finan
David Jackson
Steve Von Jasinski
Ray E. DeGraw
Keith Dufrane
James D. Egan
Maureen C. Damiani

Grandview Heights Public Library
   Board of Trustees *(left to right)* - **Page 189**

Lloyd Herd
Teri Williams
Sharon Voelker
Al Cincione
Gene King
Bob Wandel
Ed Shaudys
Painting by staff artist, Sylvia Thomas

Krema Nut Company - **Page 193**

Mike Giunta, the giant cashew in front
   (left to right)
the gourmet mix of Tiffany King
Amanda Porter
Gene King
Jacquie Russ
Brian Giunta
John Walters
David Block

Boys Varsity Wrestling Team - **Page 219**

1. Jake Mayer
2. Blake Hughes
3. Joe Wyse
4. Ben Long
5. Jordan Tabor
6. Pat Hardy
7. James Byerly
8. Johnny Vogel
9. Alex Picazzo
10. Mike Crosky
11. Nick Mehling
12. Trevor Fortin
13. Nick Barte
14. Eric Cataline
15. Richard Cotterman
16. Andrew Rosendale
17. Steve Sharrock
18. Karl Senter
19. Josh Bartholomew
20. Nick Sutter
21. Shaun Andrews
22. Ian Dodge
23. Todd Altfater
Not pictured: Corey Bable and John Sharrock

The Varsity Girls Basketball Squad - Page 217

Allie Avishai-manager
 (left to right)
Jaren Woodland
Ericca Lovegrove
Claire Nichols
Annie Avishai
Gilli Grace
Coach Steve Hall
Anna Hartenstein
Jessi Graham
Jill Elder
Jackie Jones
Anne Nichols

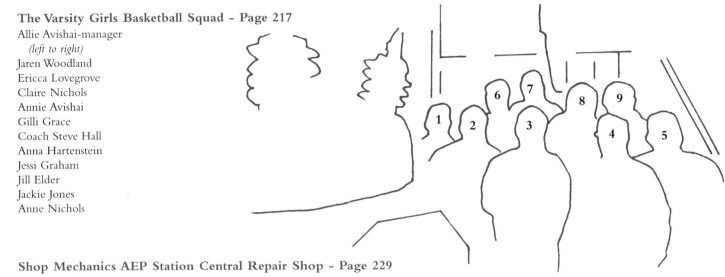

Shop Mechanics AEP Station Central Repair Shop - Page 229

1. Jerry Yoho
2. Bruce Gruenler
3. John Christian
4. Gary Knox
5. Bob Fout
6. Mark Blair
7. Rick Harden
8. Haskel Johnson
9. Rick Watterman

ACKNOWLEDGMENTS

For generations to come the year 2000 will be looked upon as a threshold. Technology, morals, clothing styles and many aspects of life will at some point be compared to this year. I hope, in the future, another photographer will pursue a similar project. Should that happen that photographer will need the help of others just as I have.

Dave Levingston and Scott Orts have been my coaching staff, cheering section and in Dave's case, under-appreciated critic. These two have believed in my project from day one. Their insight into what this project could become has been invaluable.

Mr. Jim Toms, publisher of the Tri-Village News and Mr. Craig McDonald of ThisWeek in Grandview were generous in allowing me to reprint text from their publications. Mayor Colleen Sexton of Grandview Heights and Mayor Frank Monaco of Marble Cliff have opened doors for me. School superintendent Dr. Paul Kulik gave me access to faculty, staff and students in the Grandview Heights City Schools.

Marcey Hawley of Orange Frazer Press in Wilmington, Ohio, Mike Dexter of the IDC Design Group, Inc. in Grandview, Becky DeRoads of The Millcraft Group, and Kevin Ring of Hopkins Printing have taken my rough idea and given it a finish I could not have dreamed of.

And finally, my thanks go to the people who are part of this project. They allowed me into their homes, classrooms, or meetings, stopped their busy days to make room for my camera and me and went out of their way to make these photographs possible.

Thank you, one and all.

Kenneth D. Frick